W0009375

southern atheist.
oh, honey

southern atheist. oh, honey
© d. e. fulford / Cathexis Northwest Press

No part of this book may be reproduced without written permission of the
publisher or author, except in reviews and articles.

First Printing: 2021

ISBN: 978-1-952869-32-7

Cover art by Faith D. Parks
Designed and edited by C. M. Tollefson

Cathexis Northwest Press
cathexisnorthwestpress.com

southern atheist.
oh, honey

d.e. fulford

Cathexis Northwest Press

For the outcasts, the hopeful, and the broken who clamor forth even when everything is shaking.

For my unyielding mama who never once thought I couldn't do it all.

For my HLP Amanda, BFF Missile, and every passionate, gorgeous being who loves me.

For my chosen family with so much love: Levi (29) and The Walrus.

Poems 6, 9, 11, and 14 published by *Blood Pudding Press*, November 2020

Poems 7, 10, and 12 published by *Cathexis Northwest Press*, January 2021

1.

in this humidity we can taste the lightening bugs/mama never stops telling the stories/of chubby
toddler flesh spotted bulbous in chigger bites/such insolent baby/brown-black rivulets cake my
ragged skin/what if i wasn't her first/in different parts of america they say *fireflies*/cake slices of
air won't give me cavities/kudzu only grows where it's wet/she tells me i wouldn't let her help
me walk/memories contrive by snapshots/there are zoo animals on the plane to north carolina/
shirtless in a diaper i watch feet/no wonder certain tribes deny cameras/when the ether droops
as honey is a spoonful plenty to tamp down my growing yawn emerging from within

2.

she draws my initials on the bottoms of the ponies' hooves/sun-warmed plastic smells of pastel

affection/when my aunt comes from missouri she helps my cousin cheat in the easter egg hunt/

across the street the grey woman has cheap ice cream/lizzie's curls jiggle of sunlight/black

mountain thunderstorms shake our warm room/poor white women steal from children/family is

already subjective/but my brothers come at the same time/i don mama's fedora/she places two

honeyed skulls on my pink sweatpants/this is duty of concern i never wanted so sweet so pain

3.

i realize we worship honeysuckle/pull the gentle sweetness between temporary teeth/linoleum looks like spilled marbles/birthday candle tells me the five of us are not ready for such family/my brothers and i share a bunk bed/mama tells me sometimes a person just feels like crying/slivers of wisdom effortlessly stick in malleable mind/for the first time we have a garden/the twins scream all nights/i tell mama it is a time for crying/she disagrees/the first nightmare i remember is a tiger's mouth close/from our basement apartment we live beneath the feet/she has no patience for my tears when the twins need her/and i know better/i can do this myself of course

4.

my phonics books are school bus golden/letter sticker-backs taste like cherry cough drops/i am only allowed to read if i eat/the teenager at the pool is called tammy/it is a short walk to the library/my advent calendar marks time until kindergarten begins/i quiver atop the pile of books i am set to read/tammy has scarecrow's hair she weaves flower crowns/my brothers grab sticks as we perch on wet bleachers for mama's camera/i think our seedling is a watermelon and sing it into perfect squash/the skin on our shins is whisper-thin and bruises like honeyed plum flesh

5.

at the boone house there are horses/we have to spell our names aloud each morning/i feel bad for genevieve/shannon gets in trouble at naptime for bringing matthew into the bathroom/the horses are called frank and charlie/ms. miller takes me to a special lunch and i read the menu to her/fear is high school boys on the school bus/dirt roads do not make me carsick when i am reading/ winter's impatience crashes sledding over cow hills/i hum of memory in every single dream/the loudest laugh mama feeds frank and charlie marshmallows/horse teeth cannot clutch cushiony sugar puff/she never lets us sleep without saying *good night i love you* never even once

6.

there was no ill-intent toward the bee/my foot swelled for half a day congealed inside baking soda mask/we have to move again/the fixed blocks of apartments hold friend potential/thrift store roller skates never fit right/mama is the only one at home now/papa is working *on the road*/i get a reading light for my headboard/the twins line their dresser drawers with he-man dolls/when he's home all they do is yell into darkness/later i learn honey extracts a stinger from young skin/ from the trampoline across the street we hear tasha's crying her stepdad is naked scream/ fledgling tenuous i know what happens/it will never be dark in my room ever again

7.

on tuesdays after lunch some of us are pulled into a separate room/they call us a.g./we put on a

play about pompeii pen letters in freshly-honed cursive wobbles to corporate america and take

home lists of companies to boycott because they clear-cut the precious rainforest/a catholic

family of eight moves across the street/at megan's birthday i accidentally smack another girl

instead of the piñata/papa's tender breadth soaks my tears/at lunch shannon sucks a hickey into

her arm blames the vacuum/we get caught stealing red hots from food lion/confess to cashier all

her stiff hair and blue eyes she says *oh honey*/this is not a punishment i am only scared of yelling

8.

i am learning to hate the rain/forging mama's name on my reading log makes my stomach hurt/
but not as much as getting in trouble for forgetting/being a brownie scout is horror but i like
badges and cookies/on the bus we compare notes on dirty words we don't know *fuck shithead
asshole*/my brothers trap ants and blow them up with firecrackers in halloween candy bucket/
everyone is getting phones in their rooms/wearing atheism in the south is a mark of aberration/i
costume my unintentional deviance quietly but not silent/children know more about sex than
parents fathom/sunday school does not prevent dezzy from getting pregnant at twelve

9.

on the bus i tell talia *god is a gerbil* and she cries/mary has a pet skunk/we listen to michael jackson records scour mama's anatomy books/the full world is friends/kristen lives at the top of the hill but kelly is way across town/we play kickball in adam's yard even though he has diabetes/chickenpox summer quarantine/i cry *i'm so ugly* mama says *but only right now—some people will be ugly their whole lives*/book pile is growing i've now read millions/mama's sewing machine pulses with the kitchen lights/for halloween i am a homemade bird of paradise/dressing up for "bare book night" in the cafeteria and the bird returns/kids don't always know when they are being mocked/things we never forget/mama's clay shapes/tension like wire cuts still hot

10.

no matter how much i don't want to move i can't walk away fast enough/decisions made in anger change everything/for two weeks i explore the country with papa in his eighteen-wheeler/my entire life is playing pinball in truck stops/we listen to rush limbaugh because papa likes to laugh/i am bored and count the letter "d" on billboards/i run for school president because my opponent chad whispers *yesss* to himself when he gets a good grade/it annoys me/i win the election even though i only just moved to banner elk/a lady tells mama i am going to be a news anchor in life/for north carolina this is high praise/chad's buck teeth or brown curls ask me to be his girlfriend/it is now i learn defiance is my power/i'll attract my flies with vinegar—not honey

11.

the documentary said nightmares are suppressed fears surfacing like bodies you tried to drown/in science we get $20 to pick a pet/i convince my group we need a tarantula/before i sleep i read the list of things i hate so they do not perform in my dreams/dehydrated spider skin is scratchy and sad/the whole world has a boyfriend but me/mrs. bullock makes us say where we go to church/i didn't expect social studies to be about my atheism/four kids bring worship pamphlets to next class/my divergent existence is not safe in the classroom/the walls are talking about me/in homes i'll never enter my ears decant blood thicker than cold honeycake/i just want a boy to like me/too shyly defective every thumping second/maybe a god could help me believe if i could try enough

12.

we are all products of what we eat/everyone knows conforming will make or break you/i start erecting my fortress when mama snaps off the t.v. in scowl/tears are not always wet/i gnaw past cuticles until blood splashes out/xmas lights painting the window render my honey-face palpable/she won't know i lie to the girls in class/i cuff my jeans like do-wop until whitney asks *where's the flood*/before the internet middle school was tangible pain/teenagers disparage the unfamiliar or poor/half gallon of breyer's melts soft globs the pyrenes licks away/laughter hurts/ ghosts visit in the night through the mirror above my bed/maybe one of them will be my boyfriend/i never fought harder to keep anyone/but she feeds me milk each night/and i still break

13.

a summer blossoms within my becoming/the middle school gives us planners/writing in markers is my trend/if the squared calendar dates are confessions i am a supplicant/samantha and karen keep taking me to church after sleepovers/someone keyed the cheerleading coach's car so we are benched the first game/insolence mushrooms like unhurried winter honey-drip/the list of boys who like me is longer than my name/every single thing i touch is hormone-tinged and humming/i realize too late logan wanted to kiss me at heather's party/each track event is mine/summer barks death to this burgeoning adolescent success/i cry i pack i quit eating/brevity begets perpetuity

14.

uprooted again i am the worst tree/southern friends warn colorado will turn me into a *skater*/ sometimes the worst possible thing means nothing at all/we change sheets to stay in town/my brother catches me flushing my breakfast/elk wander the golf course instead of adorning town names/the letters from back home are my blood/i offer stephen king corn nuts the night of my first kiss/this is not a euphemism/debauchery is friendlier than unsuspecting complacency/ courting peril flatters/he buys us coors light to drink under honey june bridge/when the river behind the rental cabin freezes we skate to the hockey rink/where they will always wait/joel high sticks my face/gives me kfc and punk rock as apologies but my soul is now saved

15.

missy's dad finds the list we kept/parents always think i am the mistake/a dropout sells us mistys from the u-pump-it in lyons/every single car advises tree fresheners do not stymy blue smoke memories/i consent to trying in the parking lot of st. bart's with joel/kerry and i did community service there freshman year after the suburban incident/a conman cheats us of mama/the walk to the malt shop where i work makes me sweat/now that i buy my own groceries i never forget the desserts/i waste weeks with waylon and zeb in watagua county/get fired from malt shop/every gulp of wilted youth just means we are more alive than yesterday/kerry and i sit daily on the corner waiting for world to happen/older boys riff on corner but always know just where i am

16.

bff necklaces are easy to pocket/where does missy end and i begin/we find boyfriends in out-of-town spaces/joel jokes *only real men drive hyundais* teaching me to drive a clutch in sunday's empty lot/church now is effortless/without enough time to be lonely we fill every instant with each other/find homegrown at the boulder theater/thrift vintage adidas jackets in arvada because here it's okay to wear clothes someone else owned/the offspring cycles in the toyota stereo/even when we make each other mad we sit at our table together during break/a synaptic affair could not fetch us any closer/but next year missy is going to front range and i can't plug the expanse

17.

nothing exists but firsts/i finally cry for losing mama to the conman/we eat moroccan with our
fingers in boulder feeling complex/*look how well i can still do/someday i* is not just a mantra/had
i taken foreign language i would be moving to boulder/but he is in fort collins/we recite our
future to one another in cobalt swirls of blueberry pie on ceramic/our entire town drowns in
honeysuckle/in ramskellar jimmy eat world plays for twenty people including us/ex-lovers don't
exist if you burn the evidence/he makes me cds of every show we see/my face is his as if no one
has ever seen me until now/i only this moment scald into existence/nothing this big can be real

18.

the sorority girls won't look at me during registration/they aren't rushing toward this like they want us to do them/brendy sets three alarms and never shuts them off or leaves the room/high school insistence gasps into miasma/i blow off my boyfriend for anything college/he wears a ring on his left hand/teenagers should never make promises/or think past tomorrow/when i return from cancun the colorado campus is stale milieu to my tan/some days i do nothing to stop crying/must be the reason that i'm queen of my castle/we find ecstasy at the matrix/we're boundless when the call comes/josh dies/quickly no one breathes all summer/whose god did this

19.

it is too easy to quit eating/ecstasy dusks on my sautéed sophomoric synapses/we can't smoke in

the condo i do anyway/i get the master bedroom peeling inner thigh slices in bathtub/i declare

english for a major but am too broke for a computer/street art is the gentrified version of graffiti/

poetry teacher concedes to my hesitant lyric proposal/roommate lets a boyfriend live with us for

free nags me about rent/leaves her journal open to *how much i love to hate devon*/american

yellow warbler wants in through my window/i might soon be joining it in laughing blithe prayer

20.

the golden retriever will become my best friend/it is five weeks since i quit smoking/i see his calves when they play frisbee/the way forward is not today lined with kind objectives/the conman i will never call daddy has a cabin in the woods if my boyfriend works for him/i sell my lease on nineteen blazing backward to old professions/he invites mikey to drink without asking me/the sound of belligerent splintering echoes in empty bottles/he sighs jack daniels across my sternum proposing marriage in old town/celebration is not ex-girlfriend's bed/everyone calls her *butterface*/i laugh because it is not me/our new apartment reminds me only of aging or wet sobs

21.

everyone said not to so we did/i marry a drink not a human/i'm graduating a semester early/on

mwf emily sean and i smoke with our literature professor bandying allegory of *anna karenina*

jargon/our campus bar smells lost/can poets love electricians/emily's farmhouse and fiancé both

erroneous jigsaw pieces in her swirl of fat ginger coils and vintage blouse/it's the first time i feel

ashamed of a mate/my brother casey is the only one who calls graduation day/i don't walk so no

one comes/who even lays precedence on ceremony/someone wedding-gifted fat margarita

glasses/i've memorized the bubbled pattern beneath the surface of tequila pretending i am not

22.

an alien heaviness relaxes into every limb floods my guts/with stinging alacrity i have come to trust every bottle/manager connie hates me because i am married/if she knew the way i envy steph's neck tattoo she'd weep/daytime television smears me motionless/for the first time ever i quiver/the avalanche make the stanley cup/his testosterone mimes authentic passion/on the deck at the minnesota lake house his grandma divulges she is a gypsy/nothing welcomes a nap like measured rain/i am vermicelli donning clingy lefse dress/maybe jet skis are built for weird sex/ grandma is not impressed/her clairvoyant twitching eyes know god is lying/just like me

23.

on the pond i catch more fish than the boys/ray wants to drive me back home/in my new retail universe the entire space is *fashionably late*/we probably should not have borrowed so many clothes/but rob and i run this town/we follow katy around she gives the boys sloppy haircuts/they pay her in klonopin they wish was her mouth/cheap joint smoky raucous of *shoes* and my husband rips apart his arm in counterfeit irish accent of blotto/everyone notices our sensitivity gravitas/i meet me again in dressing room mirror/designer jeans really do make your butt look better/when your lips are occupied you cry less/the chipotle manager trades in chips and salsa/if you pinched until honey squeezes from my pores i still couldn't believe how good this feels

24.

i pour myself through every dark/i left but legs are not for walking when the night never ends/in my driver's seat tomorrow looks like honeycomb/i practice saying the alphabet backward just in case/teasing is foreplay no matter how old you are/sliding through the january intersection was safer than stopping/latin men are voted most likely to comment on my calf tattoos/the second one hurt less/*shattered heart* my pious totem/maybe this is why i never stop going under the gun/of metallic hummingbird twirping forever-marks/i emerge post-dusk parched and willing/every already-uncapped pbr dissolves back a little more of the past/anyone can fall in want in starlight

25.

the shop fluorescents bite hangover skull/hiding in the dressing room eating chicken biscuits/we

got used to taking the disposable camera for personal use/an unintended professional undoing/my

wetly inked hipbone sways into his four poster the night his grandma dies/pinball neon and a

splash of urgency/shutter flashes transparency of girl child thrashing/lara works at the bank

swears to safeguard my money mugs me blind/over martinis stephen and i decide we'll fight her/

nothing left to lose is a perilous endeavor/when liquor no longer lubricates out the fear what

remains/forget flailing i am earnest sea of praying nightly swelling on barstools left salty with

my touch/heaving diffident surge-motion of living mostly afloat/weary waters never stop waving

26.

it is the year time moves backward/jim jarmusch could catch me off-key/i animate in night-stretches of screaming brain/inhaling a blind sweat-stained pillow before he comes each morning/amanda is heterosexual life partner/we swear never again to drink buttershots old fashioneds/worship *coffee and cigarettes* from the middle of the road/if i split myself open with the porch icicles might we rebuild my guts/i return from miami and his alkaline trio tattoo sits in the office/bipolar should come with warning labels/perhaps lonely eyes are illiterate/this fairytale looks possible/but with hans christian anderson gore-strewn ending disney would never abide/ mama would be proud/she wants her kids procreating/when girls in third grade said they wanted babies i told my teacher i would be an actress/guess nothing is stopping me these days

27.

we are so fragile a whisper may slay us/he has all of my favorite bands on his ipod before we

meet/every second clicks by in dance/working and living with someone can be the safest peril/in

palm desert we're the only ones alive worshipping st. valentine/it's years delayed i learn the

warning signs for such mental disease/pete casts us both in the film/road trips bend my curves

slow desert tripping until i find he's been here before/our fairy story previously penned starred a

heroine i'll never meet/his copper blood stench in my bathroom/the same night he leaves i put

the ring in a box/my students are gentle cherubs clamoring/cleft afflictions now he's in the

hospital i visited jaime there she thought she was god/my mind though is not cracked it's so sad

28.

unanimously in accord with myself 'cause i'm all that's left/the fort collins street signs are

flaking when hunter and i cartwheel in the street/faye invites me to her beach/saltwater corrupts

my cloying memory/i never had a hometown/but the road hum drinks drifters afloat and i am still

trying to believe/peas and carrots amanda and i eat flowers in old town square at midnight/

nantucket nights with pete on eight millimeters of my bourbon-gasps/anything to outflow my

living nightmare/at 70s steakhouse i'll never tell/patti lifts seasoned salt/we take kath to dirt bar

popcorn clings the sticky tabletop/honey song drags me back to coast/karaoke crying in the rain/

i'm awash i'm ready i'm begging/when i hold my breath i don't fill but i don't sink

29.

before we meet we slow-dance in your living room/thick air buoyed with cicada circus of summer patios/we linger in *one more just one more*/can home be a person/lily pads in the oriental garden retell me of your freckled shoulders/when you're falling cheap beer does not stink of desperation/one honeyed afternoon we listen to bad religion driving south on first eat sushi in a strip mall melting with time/your city becomes my need like water and your bowed mouth/austin is misty to catch us a breathless warm prayer/greenbelt bathwater lounging through midair/ summer thighs suck vinyl booth bench/our purring commingling and i'm a believer/it's a good thing i've never been terribly afraid of heights/or the color of a thousand miles away

d.e fulford is a writer and English instructor at Colorado State University. She earned master's degrees in both creative writing and education and is in her third year of her doctor of education in transformative leadership. Other poems and lyrical essays can be found in *The Dead Mule School of Southern Literature, Longridge Review, Blood Pudding Press, Indolent Books, Dreamers Magazine, Crosswinds Poetry Journal, Sunspot Literary Journal*, and many others.

She resides on the front range of the Rocky Mountains with her partner Levi and their chocolate Labrador, The Walrus. In her spare time, she can be found riding her Triumph Street Twin motorbike, attending live music shows, and advocating for conversations about topics that make us squirm.